WALMER CASTLE AND GARDENS

TOUR OF THE CASTLE BY ROWENA SHEPHERD MA
TOUR OF THE GARDENS AND GROUNDS BY VIRGINIA HINZE
HISTORY OF THE CASTLE BY JONATHAN COAD MA, FSA

Introduction

Walmer Castle was built in 1539 as one of a chain of coastal artillery forts constructed by Henry VIII against the threat of invasion by Spain. From 1708, it became the official residence of the Lords Warden of the Cinque Ports, an office held by many famous people, including the Duke of Wellington, Sir Winston Churchill and the late Queen Mother. The castle was adapted over the years by successive Lords Warden, to make it into a more comfortable home, and the grounds were developed into attractive gardens, which are still changing today.

*Victorian pot lid showing the Duke of Wellington
riding near Walmer Castle*

CONTENTS

Front cover photograph by David Sellman

*With thanks to the following people for their help and advice:
Hugh Axton, Jonathan Bailey, Jenny Charnick, Louise Dando, Maryline Dyer, Dr Michael Hoskin, Sally Mewton-Hynds, Tracey Wahdan and John Watkins.*

*Printed in England by St Ives Westerham Press
C100, 3/03, ISBN 1-85074-726-1, 03723*

Visit our website at
www.english-heritage.org.uk

CABBINS for Gunners Propoſed at *WALMER CASTLE*

The Gunners' Lodging, built in the early 1730s, from a drawing dated 1741

Right: Entrance to the Gunners' Lodging from the courtyard. The house was built for the castle gunners in the early 1730s

A photograph of the basement when it was used as a recreation and play area by the Beauchamp family in the 1930s

Turn right through the first set of doors as you leave the shop, and go down the steep stairs to the basement, using the plan on page 37 to find your way round.

Although the interior of the castle has been altered over the years, the ground floor and the basement retain much of their Tudor layout. At the bottom of the stairs, in a domed chamber, is the castle well. Surrounding it are three rib-vaulted rooms, lit by narrow splayed windows from the courtyard. These rooms were originally used for storage. The sign 'Soldier's Kitchen' on one of the doors probably relates to its use during the Napoleonic Wars.

Go back up the stairs and turn right at the top. Follow the path round past the tea rooms into the Hall Room.

The Hall Room

This Hall Room is in the part of the castle that was once the Gunners' Lodging, a two-storeyed weather-boarded structure built in the early 1730s, during the Duke of Dorset's tenure. It was one of the earliest domestic additions to the fabric of the castle. It comprises two rooms, on both ground and first floors, on either side of a central corridor. As the name indicates, the ground-floor area provided accommodation for the gunners, while the upper rooms were reserved for the use of officers.

By the 1740s, this area was no longer used to accommodate military staff. The inventories record that the Duke of Dorset's page and a cook used these rooms, and they contained beds, linen and plate.

By Pitt's time the rest of the bastion had been built over and the ground-floor rooms became dressing rooms attached to the two newly built guests rooms next door. Later, in the nineteenth century, they once again reverted to use by servants, housing the butlers and housekeepers of successive Lords Warden.

In 1939, the partitions between three of the ground-floor rooms and the hallway were removed by Lady Willingdon, the wife of the last resident Lord Warden, opening up most of the ground floor to enable free circulation during parties and other entertainments. At this time this room became the entrance hall, and contained a mixture of country house furniture of different periods. The large print, *His Last Return from Duty*, after James Glass, shows Wellington leaving Horse Guards for the last time as Commander-in-Chief of the army.

The Sackville and Willingdon Rooms

These two rooms were built in the space between the Gunners' Lodging and the bastion wall a decade or so after the Gunners' Lodging, and were recorded as being complete by 1746. They were used as extra bedrooms for visitors during William Pitt's time.

Later, Lady Granville used the Willingdon Room as her bedroom, and both rooms had large mullioned windows inserted into the casemates by George Devey, giving views onto the kitchen gardens and the moat. By 1939, when the Beauchamp family was in residence

for long periods in the summer, the Sackville Room was used a bedroom for four housemaids. The servants' bells are still in the central part of the keep, but are not on view to the public.

The Willingdon Room usually houses a number of items that are associated with William Pitt the Younger (these may be removed from display when the room is used as an exhibition area). The mahogany desk corresponds very closely with the description of one noted in the Walmer account books for 26 June 1798 ('a mahogany library table with drawers on one side and panell door with pidgionhole on other side covered with green cloath and on large casters'), costing eighteen pounds and eight shillings. The rococo style mahogany framed armchairs in the Sackville Room were also possibly part of the furnishings in Pitt's time. Likewise, the metal-framed chair by the entrance – commonly called a campaign chair, because furniture of this type could be taken apart for travelling – once belonged to Pitt.

Go up the stairs and into the first room on the left.

Top: The Sackville Room, shown hung with black crêpe during the 150th anniversary of Wellington's death in 2002

Above: William Pitt the Younger's campaign chair

Left: Servants' bells, dating from the time of Lord and Lady Willingdon in the 1940s

Cartoon of Wellington by Henry Heath, drawn in 1828, when the duke was Prime Minister and Commander-in-chief of the army

Staircase and Landing

As you go up the stairs, there is a bust of the Duke of Wellington by the Italian sculptor Peter Turnerelli on the window-sill. It was first loaned to Walmer Castle from the Royal Collection by King Edward VII in 1904. It formed part of the contents of George IV's demolished Carlton House, where it was displayed as part of the decorations of the fête held in 1814 to celebrate the Duke of Wellington's victories.

The Lucas Room

Portrait of Wellington, by Sir Thomas Lawrence, 1814, on display at Apsley House. This was one of the best-known images of the duke, reproduced on a number of items in the Lucas Collection

The Lucas Collection of Wellington memorabilia was assembled by Wing-Commander Thomas Hill Lucas (1895–1975) with great discernment, and donated by him in 1966 to the castle. The collection records the public face of the Duke of Wellington during his lifetime, and covers a wide variety of artefacts, all illustrating the enduring popularity of the 'Iron Duke'. After

THE DOUBLE DEALER.

APSLEY HOUSE/BRIDGEMAN ART LIBRARY

1815 and the Battle of Waterloo, Wellington's fame spread throughout Europe, and portraits of him were in great demand by the hero-worshipping public. After his military career had ended, Wellington went into politics and remained in the public eye through the work of engravers and caricaturists.

Besides engravings and a fine range of portrait busts of varying sizes and media, there are also humbler objects – paperweights, door-stops and transfer-printed pot lids, all stamped with his unmistakable likeness. Pot lids were a local speciality. The pots which they came from originally contained food, in particular shrimp paste. Many were produced and sold as souvenirs in seaside towns such as Whitstable. The two wall cabinets contain a fine collection of coins that are cast in a variety of metals and celebrate different aspects of the Duke of Wellington's life.

The room itself has been decorated to complement the collection. The replica wallpaper is from a mid-nineteenth-century design. The yellow moreen curtains are of a similar style to those found in the Duke of Wellington's room opposite, as is the Brussels weave carpet.

Leave this room by the same door and cross over the corridor to the opposite room.

The Duke of Wellington's Room

This room did not exist until William Pitt made his alterations to this part of the castle. Lady Hawkesbury, the wife of the subsequent Lord Warden, Lord Liverpool, described both the Lucas and Wellington rooms as 'only lately made into rooms and fitted up by Mr Pitt for a winter apartment, being much the warmest part of the Castle on act of thickness of the walls and the aspect, which is west'.

The room continued to be used by successive Lords Warden as their bedroom. But the most lasting changes were made by the Duke of Wellington. Like Pitt, he found this part of the castle to be the warmest, and set up his all-purpose sleeping and living room in here. His room was simply furnished, and much of what he used can still be seen today, but this was not always so.

Traditionally, a new Lord Warden bought the furniture and contents of the castle from his predecessor's estate, but Lord Palmerston at first declined to do this. So in order to prevent Wellington's possessions from being dispersed, the second Duke of Wellington removed his items to Apsley House for safekeeping.

W H Smith, who was appointed Lord Warden in 1891, initiated the Indenture of Heirlooms by Act of Parliament, in order to ensure the retention of historic items at Walmer.

Walmer People

THE DUKE OF WELLINGTON
(1769 – 1852)

THE ART ARCHIVE/WELLINGTON MUSEUM/EILEEN TWEEDY

A Wellington Boot, or the Head of the Army, *by Paul Pry, 1827*

The post of Lord Warden of the Cinque Ports fell vacant in 1828, and it was offered to the Duke of Wellington, who was Prime Minister at the time. (The office had been held by three Prime Ministers before.) Wellington held the post until his death twenty-four years later in 1852, and he became a familiar figure in the area, visiting every autumn.

The duke loved Walmer, in spite of its spartan appearance. He thought that it was the 'most charming marine residence', and that the lime trees in the garden were 'the finest in the world'. He regularly entertained family and friends, as well as local dignitaries. Moreover, because Walmer was close to the port of Dover, the duke often invited foreign royalty who were travelling between Britain and the Continent. One of his last official guests at Walmer was Her Imperial Highness the Grand Duchess, Catherine of Russia.

A Walk by the Sea-shore, *by John Doyle (HB), 1832*

This watercolour sketch of the Duke of Wellington's room at Walmer Castle was made shortly after his funeral, and was used to illustrate the book Apsley House and Walmer Castle, *by Richard Ford, published in 1853. It shows the placing of the furniture, which is similar to that on display today, including the chair in which the duke died*

It was in the Marquess of Dufferin and Ava's period as Lord Warden that the third Duke of Wellington proposed to return the original furnishings to the duke's room. However, the next incumbents at Walmer, Lord and Lady Salisbury were not so enamoured of the Duke of Wellington, and Lady Salisbury chose to use this room as her study.

The present appearance of the room is due to the pioneering work of Lady Reading. During her husband's brief tenure (from 1934 to 1935), she took an interest in the history of Walmer and its occupants, and attempted to recreate the room as it had been shortly after the Duke of Wellington's death, drawing on descriptions and surviving fragments. Having found a sample of wallpaper in the castle which she thought to be of the right period, Lady Reading had it copied. (The pattern does not correspond entirely with that seen in the watercolours of the duke's room but it is quite close.) The original carpet did not survive, so instead a faded fragment from Apsley House, the duke's London house, (which was

also seen in a portrait of the duke in his study at Stratfield Saye) was used as a model. The curtains were also later reproduced following the originals, which survive in a shattered state.

After this, the fourth Duke of Wellington felt able to return the contents of the room, and its current spartan appearance reflects the description of the room in the Thomas Shotter Bouys watercolour above, painted shortly after the Duke of Wellington's death.

Go through the doorway in the centre of the left-hand wall.

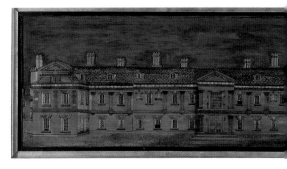

The Wellington Museum

This small room houses the Wellington Museum. The collection in the museum was acquired by Lady Reading, who gathered together items associated with the duke's tenancy at the castle as Lord Warden. The collection reflects the private life of the duke at Walmer. On display is the death mask, made by the sculptor George Gammon Adams, and a pair of the famous 'Wellington' boots.

The Duke of Wellington had become a hero in Britain, after the Battle of Waterloo. So when he instructed his shoemaker, Mr Hoby of St James Street in London, to cut the top of his boots lower, in a style that was much easier to wear with the recently introduced trousers, this form of boot immediately became fashionable, and was named after its famous wearer, the Wellington.

During the duke's time at the castle, this room was used as his dressing room, but later it was a bedroom, used by his parliamentary colleague and great friend, Arbuthnot. After his death, it was the room in which his valet, Kendal, slept.

The marquetry picture of Stratfield Saye over the chimneypiece also belonged to Wellington. It was made by the estate carpenter and displayed by Wellington at the Great Exhibition of 1851. It was a favourite piece of the duke's and during his lifetime hung in the recess in the Dining Room at Walmer Castle.

Go back across the corridor into the Pitt Museum.

Above: Wellington's boots

Marquetry picture of Stratfield Saye, the Duke of Wellington's country home in Berkshire

WELLINGTON'S DEATH AT WALMER

It was in the Duke of Wellington's room at Walmer Castle, on 14 September 1852, that the Duke of Wellington died, at the age of eighty-three. His valet, Kendal, had found him unable to stir from the small campaign bed, and had called for the local apothecary Mr Hulke. Early in the afternoon the duke was lifted from his bed to his armchair and made comfortable, but it was clear that his health was deteriorating, and he died, just before half past three.

The duke's death mask was made three days later, before his body was finally placed in its coffin. The coffin was then placed on a bier in the room, which had been cleared of its furnishings and draped in black crêpe. A guard of honour composed of a section of the duke's own regiment, the 33rd of Foot, was mounted day and night. On 9 and 10 November over 9,000 local people were allowed into the castle to pay their respects. Wellington's coffin was finally taken to London the following day, nearly two months after his death.

ILLUSTRATED LONDON NEWS

The Duke of Wellington's room at Walmer during his lying-in-state, from the Illustrated London News, *1852*

Above: Bronze death mask of the Duke of Wellington

Portrait of William Pitt the Younger, by Gainsborough-Dupoint, 1790s

The Pitt Museum

This room was originally part of the first floor of the Gunners' Lodgings, and was part of the officers' quarters during the Duke of Dorset's time. Later, during Pitt's time, it was a dressing room to the guest bedroom in the Lucas Room.

The room now contains the castle's collection of memorabilia relating to William Pitt the Younger, notably part of the set of satinwood armchairs and a leather-covered library or gaming chair. On the floor is an ingrain carpet, woven after a nineteenth-century pattern, as are the dimity curtains. Both are types of furnishings recorded as having been used by Pitt at Walmer and Holmwood, his country house, which he was forced to give up in 1803 for financial reasons, when he moved permanently to Walmer.

Opposite: The corridor and the central lantern

The Pitt Museum

The display cabinet contains a few items associated with Pitt's father, Pitt the Elder, Earl of Chatham, given by his niece, Miss Madelaeine Pitt-Taylor and by Lord Curzon. The walls are hung with a selection of prints and cartoons relating to Pitt, and an oil portrait of Pitt by Gainsborough-Dupoint.

Turn left along the corridor as you leave the room.

Corridor

The corridor, that runs the full length of the castle, was created by William Pitt the Younger. Prior to this there was only one section of corridor, running from the central lantern to the Dining and Drawing Rooms. When Pitt joined the Gunners' Lodgings to the central section of the castle, he added a bridging section between the two and ran this section of corridor through to the central lantern, which contained a spiral staircase to the floors below, joining the two halves. In the second half of the nineteenth century, the Granvilles had this staircase removed, and they painted the corridor a 'soft Morris blueish green'. (It had previously been painted to imitate oak panelling.) This colour was maintained by their successors with little variation and it has been restored after microscopic analysis of paint cross-sections.

The collection of prints in the corridor reflects the many influences on the interiors at Walmer. Those in heavy gilt frames in the lantern were in the Drawing Room in Wellington's time, but had been moved to their current position by the 1890s.

In the section of corridor between the Wellington and Pitt Museums, there are three framed 'heirloom' lists and a fine mezzotint of W H Smith, who was responsible for the survival of so many of the heirloom items.

By the windows is a series of plans and elevations collected and given by Lord Curzon, which illustrates the many phases of building at Walmer. The top-lit central section, known as the lantern, was created by George Devey for the Granvilles and is hung with prints of Wellington, George IV and other monarchs. Further along the corridor, on the left, hang photographs of the twentieth-century Lords Warden.

THE RIGHT HONORABLE
WILLIAM PITT THE YOUNGER
(1759–1806)

When William Pitt accepted the Lord Wardenship he was thirty-four and had been Prime Minister for nearly nine years. He was the first commoner to accept the post. He was in debt at the time, and since the post came with a residence and a salary of £3,000 per annum, it had become a lucrative political sinecure.

William Pitt as Colonel-Commandant of the Cinque Ports Volunteers, by Hubert, 1804

For almost the entire period of Pitt's Lord Wardenship, Britain was at war with France, starting with the declaration of war by France on 1 February 1793 and finishing with the Battle of Trafalgar on 21 October 1805. Pitt saw it as one of his principal duties as Lord Warden to protect the Kent coast from invasion. Consequently, one of his first acts was to raise a local militia, the Cinque Ports Volunteers.

It seems that Pitt had also attempted to create the eighteenth-century equivalent of an early warning system at the castle. In 1799 he received a reflecting telescope by William Herschel, the Astronomer Royal, so that he could watch for an invading fleet. However, it had been dismantled so that it could be transported safely. George Canning was at the castle when it first arrived, and attempted to assemble it, but was only able to complete two of the six steps. Two weeks later, Pitt himself attempted to follow the instructions, but it proved beyond the skills of these two eminent men.

Turn right into the Prince Consort's room.

The Prince Consort's Room

The first written reference to this room is probably a description of a room in the castle in a letter written by Lady Hawkesbury, the wife of Lord Liverpool. 'He has given me for my private room what was Mr Pitt's Library, and where there are only empty shelves – this room looks to the ramparts and over it to the sea.' This room became Lady Hawkesbury's morning room and Queen Victoria's room next door acted as her bedroom.

By the Duke of Wellington's time it was probably the room described as a 'small Sitting-room, formerly used by the Duke as his small Dining room, facing South-east, which contains the portraits of Lord Nelson, Lord North, William Pitt, George IV, Lord Thurlow, George I, Lord Liverpool, Earl of Mansfield, Lord Hawkesbury and others'.

This room, along with Queen Victoria's room next door, was altered when they became part of the royal bedroom suite during Queen

Miniature of Prince Albert, by Henry Pierce Bone, 1842; and Queen Victoria, by William Essex, c.1839

Victoria and Prince Albert's month-long visit to Walmer in 1842, with their two eldest children. The Duke of Wellington, who was Lord Warden at the time, moved out and stayed at the Ship Hotel in Dover.

It was at this time that the Prince Consort's room was divided into two, and it might have acted as a dressing room or a bedroom for the queen's dressers. During the Lord Wardenship of Lord Willingdon, the Prince Consort's room had its partition removed and was turned into a guest bedroom, with an adjoining bathroom made in one of the window embrasures.

Walk through into the next room.

Queen Victoria's Room

Queen Victoria's room was the royal couple's bedroom. Originally this room only had one window embrasure, and what is now an open balcony was a staircase to the ground floor. This room was first altered when the Duke of Dorset's extension was built onto the first floor of the castle, around 1735, making it part of his private apartments.

The way the bed partition is placed in this room, dividing it into two areas, one for the bed

and one for the dressing room, is typical of a late eighteenth-century bed recess. This indicates that it is likely to have acted as a bedroom from that time. When the royal couple stayed, however, this arrangement was changed and the bed was placed in the main part of the room, and the curtained-off alcove acted as a dressing room.

Wellington leaving Walmer for the Ship Hotel, by John Doyle (HB), 1842

Queen Victoria and Prince Albert walking along the beach at Walmer from the Illustrated London News, *25 November 1842*

COUNTRY LIFE PICTURE LIBRARY

Queen Victoria's room in 1919, pictured in Country Life

Furniture was specially brought in for the visit, but very little of this now survives, apart from the armchair, the chaise-longue in the Prince Consort's room and the four-poster bed. The armchair and chaise-longue are now covered in a copy of a chintz, found by Lady Beauchamp, which shows Queen Victoria's profile and that of the Prince Consort among small bunches of flowers. The bed was moved and cut down by later Lords Warden, as Lady Granville confessed in a letter to Lord Curzon: 'We were Goths enough to cut it down to a half-tester, but must plead as excuse that it was a hideous object with curtains and deep valence and canopy, all in yellow moreen with a woollen fringe.' The present chintz hangings, much

faded, date from around 1900 when Lady Salisbury returned the bed to the room and refurbished it. The prints of Queen Victoria and the Prince Consort were given as heirlooms by Lord Salisbury, though Lady Granville notes that they were given to her husband by Queen Victoria on a visit to Balmoral Castle.

Throughout the later nineteenth and twentieth centuries, Queen Victoria's room remained the principal bedroom of the Lords Warden, until the evacuation of the castle in 1939 at the outbreak of the Second World War. It is currently shown as it was during the Beauchamp's tenure.

Go back out into the corridor and turn right.

Walmer People

W H SMITH
(1825–1891)

William Henry Smith was a member of the publishing family who brought the first newsagents to railway stations. He is also known for having been satirised in Gilbert and Sullivan's operetta H M S Pinafore as the First Lord of the Admiralty who attained his position, despite never going to sea, by 'polishing up the knocker on the big front door' of the Admiralty.

When he was appointed Lord Warden in 1891, he was the then Leader of the House of Commons, but he was in poor health. He came down to Walmer in August to stay for the summer, and died here on 7 October 1891.

During his brief tenure he took a great interest in Walmer's history, and was particularly keen to prevent the removal of items connected with the castle's history (as nearly happened in the case of some of Wellington's possessions). Traditionally each Lord Warden bought the contents of the castle at a given price, with a sum deducted for wear and tear. These items then became the Lord Warden's personal property. Smith proposed to establish items with historical associations as heirlooms, which could not be removed from Walmer. He drafted an Act of Parliament detailing the conditions and describing the items in question, stipulating that a framed list was to be hung in the corridor.

Theatre poster for H M S Pinafore, in which W H Smith was satirised as the First Lord of the Admiralty who had never been to sea

W H Smith died before he was able to implement the act, and it was left to his son, W F D Smith, with the agreement of the Marquess of Dufferin and Ava, Smith's successor as Lord Warden, to complete the formalities. Lady Granville, the wife of Smith's predecessor, had always been very interested in the history of Walmer and in 1892 was allowed by Lord Dufferin to attach small, brass, numbered plates to identify the heirloom items. (Many of these can still be seen today.)

The framed list of Walmer Castle heirlooms

Right: The deed box containing the Act of Parliament listing the Walmer heirlooms

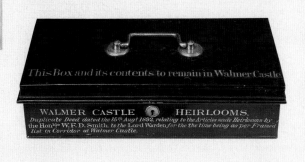

Portrait of H M Queen Elizabeth the Queen Mother, by John Gilroy, c.1950s

The Drawing Room, displayed as it was in the 1920s and 1930s

The Ante Room

The Ante Room and the adjoining Dining and Drawing Rooms were built in the 1730s as part of the Duke of Dorset's alterations to the castle, which were made in order to create a set of inhabitable rooms for his own use. There were originally four small rooms overlooking the bastion here, but by 1785 a visitor credits Pitt with having removed a partition and altered the fireplaces in order to create a large Drawing Room. Pitt may also have been responsible for the panelling, and for removing two windows on the far wall of the Dining Room, which were replaced by the niche in which the sideboard stands, thus creating the two principal entertaining rooms in the castle. All three rooms have panes of tinted glass, which are thought to have been put in by Lord Liverpool, for the comfort of his wife, whose eyes were troubled by strong light. The Ante Room contains part of a set of fine views of the castle, as well as pictures of Dover and Deal from the 1730s.

The Dining Room

The Dining Room is shown as it was used by the late Lord Warden, HM the Queen Mother, with the dining table laid for a meal. The celeste blue Minton service on the table was the one which HM the Queen Mother kept at Walmer Castle. The monograms on the plates indicate that it once belonged to the wife of Edward VII, HM Queen Alexandra. The dining table and the set of thirteen mahogany dining chairs belonged to William Pitt. They were originally cane-seated with squab cushions, but in the 1860s Lady Granville had them upholstered in the existing red morocco for use as dining chairs.

The large collection of prints in here was assembled by Lord Granville, and provides portraits of most of the Lords Warden. They are hung as they were in the nineteenth century, with the earliest to the left of the chimneypiece. In the piers between the windows are prints and photographs of the nineteenth-century Lords Warden.

The Drawing Room

The Drawing Room is displayed as it looked in the 1920s and 1930s, when the castle was used as a residence by Lord Beauchamp, who spent extended summer holidays here with his large family. It is clear that it was still very much a family home, from the frequent references in the accounts to repairs to furniture. There is a fine set of late eighteenth-century painted beechwood furniture, comprising a sofa, armchairs and window seats. The two anonymous seventeenth-century oil paintings show different views of Dover Castle.

Go through the opening to the left of the fireplace in the Ante Room and out onto the bastion to get a view of the sea and the Tudor battlements. From the bastion, follow the wall of the keep round to the right of the steps leading to the ground floor. To reach the gardens, go back through the Hall Room and straight out onto the bridge that crosses the moat.

Right: The Dining Room, laid with the celeste blue Minton service used by the Queen Mother at Walmer

Walmer Castle sits at the base of the chalk escarpment of Hawkshill Down, where it dips below the level of the shingle beach. The soils are well drained, shallow and chalky but with associated deeper loamy or clayey, flinty areas. The rainfall averages almost half that of Manchester or Cornwall. Although the castle's position exposes it to salt-laden winds, average winter temperatures remain above freezing and the shelterbelts and walls create a maritime microclimate protected from the south-westerly wind that is ideal for a wide variety of plants to flourish.

Right: Part of the survey plan drawn up in 1859 by Captain R E Scott for the War Office (scale 1:500). This was the most accurate record of the grounds until 1980

An evergreen or Holm oak in Castle Meadow

JUDITH DOBIE

Holm Oak

History of the Gardens

The present layout of the gardens is largely the result of the personal enthusiasm of two Lords Warden – William Pitt the Younger (Lord Warden from 1792 to 1806) and Earl Granville (Lord Warden from 1865 to 1890). When Pitt took up residence, the extent of the garden was limited to 'the Governor's garden', a utilitarian oblong occupying the present kitchen garden and almost certainly performing the same function. A few trees and low shrubs, or perhaps vegetables, can be glimpsed in the right-hand corner of the view by Buck made in 1735 (see page 31). A similar garden was attached to nearby Deal Castle.

Pitt was delighted with Walmer and in 1798 was 'beautifying his place with great taste'. His family were amateur but influential landscape improvers. His father created gardens with his friend 'Capability' Brown at Burton Pynset in Dorset and his uncle by marriage, Lord Temple, was busy improving the great landscape garden at

Stowe. The additional land which Pitt leased established the boundaries of the grounds as they are today. Although he does not seem to have drawn any plans, descriptions of his and Lady Hester's work by the next Lord Warden, Lord Liverpool, suggest that he at least began the plantations and laid out the kitchen garden,

PUBLIC RECORD OFFICE (MPHH 1/626)

16

the glen and perhaps the walled garden too. A survey made later in 1859 shows the shelterbelt plantations, the double ovals of the lawn and paddock, the glen, the kitchen and walled gardens and the castle meadows all well established.

Lord Granville was the other chief influence on the character of the gardens today. Unlike Pitt, though, on his appointment in 1865 he engaged a professional landscape gardener, William Masters, who ran both the Exotic Nursery in Canterbury and a successful landscaping practice. Pitt's planting had apparently matured to the point of being so overgrown that Lady Granville wrote later that 'the lawn was choked up with trees and shrubs...it was in consequence dark and damp

and unattractive'. Masters' proposals 'for the reinstatement of the grounds at Walmer' included thinning out trees on the lawn and in the belts and creating the yew-lined Broadwalk and the grassed terraces beyond. His design was inspired by the fashion for reviving the seventeenth-century, formal, Italian-style gardens of terraces and long vistas, similar to those being laid out, though on a much grander scale, by Lord Granville's cousin, the Duke of Sutherland, at Cliveden in Buckinghamshire.

The last Lord Warden to make any significant alteration to the gardens was Lord Beauchamp. He and his wife, Lady Lettice Grosvenor, sister of the Duke of Westminster, were leading lights in fashionable London society and occasionally used Walmer for

The lower terrace in high summer invites a game of croquet, or just the chance to sit and watch

Photograph of Lord and Lady Beauchamp enjoying the flower borders in the Broadwalk in the 1920s

The statue of Mercury in the Paddock

JUDITH DOBIE

Statue of Mercury

Photograph of the 'keyhole' cut by Lord Beauchamp as a focus for the Broadwalk vista; the trees have since grown and closed over it

entertainment. They played tennis in the walled garden and created another tennis and croquet lawn by recutting the grass terraces. Perhaps remembering a similar feature at his mother's family home at Chevening, Lord Beauchamp extended the Broadwalk's axis south-west to the boundary. He strengthened it visually with the two sets of steps in the grass banks and the statue of Mercury and cut a 'keyhole' in the woodland belt at the far end to draw the eye. A photograph of around 1920 shows the effect of the 'keyhole' which has now been lost.

The most recent addition to the grounds came in 1997 when a new garden was presented to Her Majesty Queen Elizabeth the Queen Mother, to commemorate her tenure as Lord Warden and to celebrate her ninety-fifth birthday. It was designed by Penelope Hobhouse, and was built within the nineteenth-century walled garden.

There is no formal route around the gardens. Visitors are invited to stroll from one part to another using the bird's-eye view on the inside front cover as a guide. The numbers in brackets refer to the labels on the bird's-eye view, and signs in the gardens.

JUDITH DOBIE

Pear tree in Moat.

Espaliered pear tree growing against the castle wall in the moat

The Moat (8)

The timber bridge that spans the moat was probably built in Pitt's time. The dry moat is one of the most sheltered parts of the garden. It is planted with spring bulbs, a range of trees and shrubs for early summer colour and hardy fuchsias for later. The walls provide warmth for fruit trees. The pear trees may originate from scions taken from trees planted by the Duke of Wellington who used the moat as a kitchen garden. Curtains of Boston ivy (*Parthenocissus tricuspidata veitchi*), which is brilliant red in autumn, a fig and a *Magnolia grandiflora*, which flowers throughout the summer with fragrant, cream, waxy flowers, all survive from Lord Granville's time and thrive on the warm walls. To the right, looking down from the bridge, is the pink 'Rosa La Follette' and, in early summer on the landward side above the moat wall, a drift of white Arum lilies (*Zantedeschia aethiopica*). Also to the right is a ramp winding its way up the face of the western outer wall, which provided access for the lawn-mowers when they were drawn by ponies. In dry weather, the shadow of a serpentine path laid out in the mid-nineteenth century and later grassed over can be seen snaking along the floor of the moat.

JUDITH DOBIE

Lime Tree

The Oval Lawn (5)

The Oval Lawn lies at the heart of the garden. It is rather like an immense 'green theatre', with a collection of fine trees, some of which are the oldest in the gardens. Its oval shape and planting is clearly shown on the 1859 survey, although the shape was somewhat flattened in the 1860s by the straight line of the yew hedge forming the back of the Broadwalk. The *Gardeners' Chronicle* magazine reported in 1898 that Pitt planted the lime trees and the yews. The top was blown out of the large lime in October 2002 but it will be kept for its historical and ecological value. Commemorative trees were planted by most subsequent Lords Warden and include two tulip trees (*Liriodendron tulipifera*), a holly (*Ilex aquifolium*) and a sweet chestnut (*Castanea sativa*) planted by Lord Rosebery in 1914. The lawn is an elegant setting for concerts and events but equally inviting for quiet picnics or reading.

JUDITH DOBIE

Tulip Tree

The Broadwalk (1)

The immense, sombre yew hedges create a perfect foil for the predominantly pastel shades of the Broadwalk's double herbaceous border. It is most colourful in the summer, when groups of plants mirror each other in repeat patterns down its eighty-metre length. The frequent clumps of day lilies (*Hemerocallis*) represent many unusual cultivars, while later in the season, tall purple and white flower spikes of 'Bear's Breeches' (*Acanthus mollis*) complement purple verbena (*Verbena bonariensis*) and sedums. William Masters carved the Broadwalk out of the Oval Lawn on one side and the southern part of the kitchen garden on the other. His original sketch for the borders in 1866 shows ribbons and zig-zags of flowers interplanted with rows of standard roses and edged with a grass strip, with the yew hedges tightly clipped. Fashions changed in the early twentieth century and in about 1916, perhaps influenced by the looser planting styles favoured by the gardener and writer Gertrude Jekyll, Earl Beauchamp replanted the beds as herbaceous borders. Helped by a particularly heavy snowfall in 1947 and from then on by clipping which exaggerated their gradually expanding undulations, the hedges have acquired a highly animated and picturesque personality.

The Broadwalk today, with its immense yew hedges and flower borders, drawing the eye to the sundial and the statue of Mercury

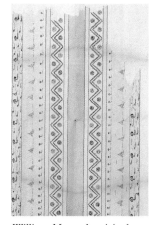

William Masters's original design for the Broadwalk border, which had flowers arranged in ribbons and zigzags

planting, which merges with the surrounding woodland, was begun in the 1860s by Lord Granville. The fine Holm oaks (*Quercus ilex*) were probably his work although William Masters had recommended planting a complete *pinetum* of 120 species. The grass is now managed as a wildflower meadow, cut twice a year. Drifts of naturalised daffodils in spring are followed by the main display of wild flowers, including pyramid orchids, yellow rattle and snakes head fritillaries, then later in the year by carpets of pink cyclamen (*Cyclamen hederifolium*) and autumn crocus (*Colchicum autumnale*).

'Rosa Queen Mother' provides the foreground to a view from the terraces back towards the Broadwalk and castle

Right: Crocuses flowering in the Paddock

The Terraces (2)

Steps lead the walk up and across two levels of grassed terraces framed by magnificent trees including a copper beech (*Fagus sylvatica atropurpurea*) and a robinia (*Robinia pseudoaccacia*). William Masters originally designed the terraces as integral parts of his formal 'Italianate' theme, with the lower terrace as a trapezium. Lord Beauchamp later broadened it to its present, more convenient rectangle for tennis, but it was always used for games and croquet is still played here today. The upper terrace retains its original curved form and annual bedding which now incorporates 'Rosa Queen Mother', a good patio and disease-resistant rose. The armillary sundial was erected in 2000 as a 100th birthday present to Her Majesty Queen Elizabeth the Queen Mother.

The Paddock (3)

The walk continues on through the paddock, which is planted informally with a range of trees and shrubs. The 1859 survey on page 16 shows its original design as a larger version of the Oval Lawn with an open, park-like character and a sharply defined edge. The present, denser

JUDITH DOBIE

The Sundial

The armillary sundial on the upper terrace beyond the Broadwalk

The Woodland Walk (10)

A circular walk winds through the perimeter woodland enclosing the paddock. Dating back to the late eighteenth and early nineteenth centuries, the tree belts were planted to shelter the new gardens from the prevailing south-westerly winds. Species are predominantly beech, lime and horse-chestnut with an understorey of yews and hollies, although these last have been drawn up by the shade of the canopy above. Sadly, its location made the shelterbelt particularly vulnerable to the two great storms of 1987 and 1990, which destroyed much of the mature tree cover. Replacement trees have been planted since, but it will take decades to restore a balanced age range of trees. Late winter is a good time to enjoy the forms and bark textures of the trees, snowdrops and, a little later, bluebells.

The Glen (4)

From the western end of the woodland walk, there is a tantalising glimpse through the tangled tree canopy down into the steep-sided glen, its woodland floor carpeted with ivy and ferns. The glen was a worked-out chalk quarry when Lady Hester wrote of her idea of 'filling the chalk pit with creepers, furze (gorse) and broom and anything that will grow to make it less barren'. Although its winding paths are not recorded until the 1859 survey, Lady Hester certainly invented the name 'the glen' and had it planted. In the longer term, it is planned to thin the seedling trees so that the picturesque character of the glen can be better appreciated from above.

The Kitchen Garden (7)

This garden has probably been in continuous production for nearly 300 years, growing fruit, vegetables and flowers, although the varieties grown today reflect ornamental rather than productive qualities. The enclosure is the oldest part of Walmer's gardens and, apart from the slice taken for the Broadwalk, retains more or less its mid-eighteenth-century shape and path system. The various box-edged compartments contain flowers for cutting, such as the old-fashioned auricular-eyed Sweet Williams, Shasta daisies and salvias. Flowers decorate the castle throughout the seasons. (The building's fabric and collections are monitored for any potential

damage from insect pests, but this is kept to a minimum by rigorous housekeeping practices.) Unusual and striking varieties of organically grown vegetables are displayed in eye-catching patterns, which change each year. Espaliered fruit trees, including pear varieties 'William' and 'Beurre Hardy', line the walks and form a small orchard at the western end. At the top of the ramp into the moat, a magnificent foxglove tree (*Paulownia tormentosa*) displays a profusion of purple flowers in May.

Willow work tunnel arbours criss-cross the rows of ornamental vegetables in a typical display, which changes each year

Autumn harvest of pumpkins and gourds in the kitchen garden

The eastern glasshouse displays plants with contrasting textures and scents and a collection of ferns

The classical pavilion reflected in the still waters of the pool in the Queen Mother's garden

The Glasshouses (7)

The eastern of the two houses was restored in 2002. It displays plants suitable for a cold greenhouse (5°–10°C) and with distinctive and contrasting forms, leaf textures and scents, which are of particular interest in winter. The easternmost compartment specialises in ferns and seasonal colour. The western house will be restored in 2003. There has almost certainly been glass in the garden from the mid-eighteenth century, although specific references to a vinery, fern-house and greenhouse do not occur until 1898. The cottages occupy the site of the former stables.

Walmer People

LADY HESTER STANHOPE
(1776 – 1839)

MARY EVANS PICTURE LIBRARY

Lithograph of Lady Hester Stanhope in oriental dress, by R J Hamerton

Lady Hester was born in 1776, the eldest of the three daughters of Charles, third Earl of Stanhope by his first wife, a sister of William Pitt. She was never financially secure, describing herself as a 'poor gentlewoman'. She lived at Walmer from 1803 until her uncle's death in 1806 and devoted great energy to improving the garden for him. She successfully persuaded the Dover Militia to turf and plant shrubs and flowers for her and Lord Guildford to give her 'a great many trees and shrubs'. Her rooms above the bridge over the moat would have given her a bird's-eye view of the gardens.

From 1810, an extraordinary career as an adventuress took her to the Mediterranean, the Middle East and north Africa. She wore Turkish or Arabian dress and was received by rulers as an equal. From 1817, she lived in a deserted monastery, Dar Djoun, in Lebanon, became a recluse and studied the occult. She died there in poverty in 1839.

Her Majesty Queen Elizabeth the Queen Mother's Garden (6)

One of the best views of the Queen Mother's garden is from the castle ramparts where its distinct forms – influenced by both classical and Islamic garden traditions – can best be seen. Its focus is a central, still pool set in a lawn and overlooked by a classical pavilion at the north end and a raised, ivy-covered viewing mound at the south end. Below the mound, a little evergreen parterre reveals two capital 'E's for Elizabeth. Broad borders provide a frame where planting changes but always reflects the Queen Mother's favourites – pastel pinks and blues. Recently, heavily scented *Lilium regale* and *Lilium* 'Pink Perfection', along with allium varieties and scented roses, have been introduced. The walls, probably erected in the nineteenth century, create a gentle microclimate, despite winter winds, which would also have favoured its nineteenth-century use as an additional kitchen garden with an orchard and trellis-covered arbours.

Castle Meadow (9)

The low-lying meadow, which was once covered by the sea, is now the only stretch of open country separating Walmer from Deal. It has a park-like character and the grassland supports typical chalk-loving species, which are maintained by sheep grazing. The most striking feature is the avenue of Holm oak clumps (*Quercus ilex*) planted in 1866 to frame what was, until about 1950, the main drive into the castle. Several replacement clumps have been planted in between the originals to maintain the design for the future. The wind-sheared trees scattered along the iron fenceline and the clumps either side of the present entrance drive are remnants of nineteenth-century shelterbelts partly replanted in the twentieth century.

JUDITH DOBIE

Avenue of Holm Oaks

Although its exterior has been softened and its interior made more comfortable after nearly 300 years as the residence of the Lords Warden of the Cinque Ports, Walmer is unmistakably a Henrician artillery fort. Dominating the centre is the great circular keep, originally surrounded – as can still be seen, unaltered, at neighbouring Deal Castle – by an open courtyard within a concentric curtain wall. Projecting from the curtain wall are four squat, rounded bastions. The northern bastion incorporates the gatehouse, leading to a drawbridge across the moat. The moat itself has a stone-faced counterscarp or outer wall, and was later divided by a couple of cross-walls added in the nineteenth century to make it into a garden. But however tranquil Walmer now looks, its construction in the politically turbulent 1530s was a response to a very real threat of invasion.

The Invasion Scare of 1539

In mid-March 1539, King Henry VIII rode through Kent to the old fortress of Dover Castle. He was anxious to inspect defences being prepared against a possible invading army, intent on overthrowing him and reinstating the authority of the Roman Catholic Church.

At this time, Henry had been on the throne for thirty years. Nine years earlier, a grateful Pope had awarded him the resounding title 'Defender of the Faith', which was retained by all subsequent British monarchs, for his book repudiating the new Protestant beliefs of Martin Luther. Henry had long sought to make England important in European affairs, using a combination of diplomacy, bribery and occasionally force. A cornerstone of his foreign policy had always been to ensure that the great Catholic powers of Spain and France never united in opposition to England. But by 1539, much had changed. Desperate for a son and heir, Henry had finally divorced his first wife, Catherine of Aragon in 1533 and married Anne Boleyn. This royal action led directly to England dismissing the authority of the Roman Catholic Church and to the English Reformation. Both the Pope and Catholic Europe were horrified, while the Emperor Charles V of Spain had personal cause for annoyance as Catherine was his aunt. In 1536, Henry began the suppression of the English monasteries, appropriating most of the wealth to the Crown.

One of a number of designs for artillery forts for the Kent coast produced around 1539

Initially, fortune favoured Henry, since France and Spain were at war. But in June 1538, Francis I of France and the Emperor Charles V made peace. A few months later, the Pope excommunicated Henry VIII. The Catholic powers were now apparently united, and a papal Bull of excommunication provided them with the justification, indeed the duty, of ridding England of its heretical king.

Preparations to Resist Invasion

By the time Henry arrived at the Kent coast on 16 March, he had already taken steps to strengthen his kingdom. Earlier, orders had been issued to ready the fleet, musters of able-bodied men were held, and the chain of warning beacons round the coast was repaired. In Antwerp and Hamburg the king's agents were recruiting mercenaries and buying extra weapons.

With a small royal navy, Henry could not rely on an invasion being defeated at sea. In February 1539, he sent out commissioners to survey the southern coasts for fortifications to protect likely landing places, dockyards, harbours and the fleet anchorages. Their reports led to the construction between 1539 and 1543 of a chain of defences running from Hull round the south coast to Milford Haven. Nothing on this scale had been attempted since the Roman forts of the Saxon Shore had been constructed more than 1200 years earlier. Like the Roman system, Henry's forts were built to a common design and financed by the State, using not just the wealth generated by the selling of the monasteries, but in many cases the actual stones torn from their buildings.

The Design of Walmer

By 1500, the introduction of heavy guns had made most existing defences obsolete. Continental countries with vulnerable land frontiers led the way in developing new and radically different designs of artillery fortifications. These were characterised by low but massive curtain walls, usually backed by substantial earth ramparts to provide extra strength and space for guns. Projecting from the curtain walls at regular intervals were bastions with guns, designed to protect the front of the defences. These bastions were either semicircular, as at Walmer, which allowed for more guns but which had 'dead ground' at their base where enemy troops could shelter, or angled, where the arrow shape allowed no 'dead ground' but meant that there were fewer weapons on the bastion.

In 1539, the design adopted for the king's fortification programme was based on a central, circular gun-tower or keep, with lower, semicircular bastions symmetrically arranged round it, allowing the mounting of several tiers of guns of different calibres. The size of the castle and the number of bastions could be varied according to local circumstances. If comparatively unsophisticated compared to some of the new angle-bastion defences then under construction on mainland Europe, Henry's fortresses were robust and would have been capable of resisting attack.

A drawing of neighbouring Deal Castle, by the Buck Brothers. Deal is a similar shape to Walmer, with a circular keep surrounded by an open courtyard and a concentric curtain wall

Aerial view of Walmer, showing its shape and its coastal position

Portrait of Henry VIII, by Holbein, c.1536–7 (detail). Of all the Tudor monarchs, Henry VIII was the most talented and prolific builder, playing a significant part in the design of fortifications such as Walmer

NATIONAL PORTRAIT GALLERY, LONDON

The Castles of the Downs: Walmer, Deal and Sandown

For centuries, the Downs has been a favourite anchorage. This sheltered stretch of water protected by the Goodwin Sands has deep water close inshore, making it easy for ships to land and embark cargoes and passengers. In 1520, the Emperor Charles V had sailed from here after his visit to Henry at Canterbury, while Henry VIII would have been well aware that Perkin Warbeck's invasion force had chosen to land here in 1495. The priority in 1539 was to protect the stretch of beach between the Sandwich Flats to the north and the Dover cliffs to the south.

Henry's officials proposed three substantial castles: Sandown, Deal and Walmer. In between these they sited four earth bulwarks or gun batteries, apparently linking all seven defence works by a defensible trench or covered way, running for some two and a half miles. The tactical siting of these defences was excellent, covering the whole length of the shore. The defensible trench, perhaps not surprisingly, had a short life and no trace of it has been found. The four bulwarks, however, survived into the eighteenth century, although long disused. Sandown Castle, partly destroyed by the sea, was almost completely demolished in the

A photograph of Sandown Castle around 1860, before the castle was largely demolished to prevent it falling into the sea

DOVER MUSEUM

mid-nineteenth century, although part of its central tower remains embedded in modern sea defences. Deal and Walmer Castles both retain much of their Tudor form.

Work began on these defences in April 1539. Records indicate that the king's officials overseeing construction had all come from supervising works at the king's palaces at Hampton Court and Nonsuch. Perhaps as a result of the king's visit to Dover (there is no record that he then came to the Downs), building proceeded at great speed with some 1400 workmen employed by the beginning of

A painting of the three 'castles in the Downs' in the early eighteenth century. Walmer is on the right with Deal towards the centre and the largely vanished Sandown beyond it

May. Deal, often referred to as the 'Great Castle', as it was the largest of the three, was sufficiently advanced by the end of the year to host a banquet for Anne of Cleves, who landed at Deal on her way to marry Henry VIII. By September 1540, construction was finished and the following month all three castles were garrisoned. An early eighteenth-century oil painting of the three castles, shown above, clearly shows not only how they dominated the shoreline before the urban growth of Deal and Walmer, but also gives a vivid impression of the concentration of sailing vessels that used the Downs.

Walmer Castle in the Sixteenth Century

In October 1540 the brand new fortress at Walmer was put in the charge of a captain, with a lieutenant, ten gunners, four soldiers and two porters. They were all quartered in the central tower or keep, and formed the trained nucleus of the garrison. In times of hostility, they would have been joined by extra men, probably recruited locally.

The Tudor gatehouse heightened by the architect George Devey in the mid-1870s to provide additional accommodation for Earl Granville

The original Tudor garrison of 1540 was there to man a bewildering number of gun positions. At basement level, a gallery running round the castle had thirty-two firing loops for hand-weapons covering the moat. The garrison had access to this gallery through a sally-port beneath the drawbridge. Above were a further three tiers of gun positions. As first constructed, each of the main bastions was hollow, with a timber platform just below parapet level. At ground level were three gun-ports, with four parapet embrasures overhead. The exception was the gatehouse, where the gateway replaced the central gun-port. In the parapet of the curtain wall, between each bastion, was a further embrasure, while the central keep may have had up to a further eight gun emplacements. In all, there were probably positions for some thirty-nine heavy weapons, although it is very doubtful if this number was ever installed. Nothing is known about the original armament. It is likely that the main weapons would have been a mixture of brass and cast-iron guns of varying sizes and calibres. The largest, a cannon of eight-inch calibre, could fire a 60lb-shot to an extreme range of some 2000 yards, while the smallest, the falconet, could fire a pound shot over a shorter range. For closer defence, the garrison was probably provided with arquebuses, fired either through the ports covering the moat, or through the parapet embrasures. Bows and arrows would also have been part of the armoury. A 1597 list of weapons at Walmer mentions one cannon, one culverin, five demi-culverins, a saker, a minion and a falcon. Apart from the cannon and the culverin, these were all small weapons, but in their method of operation they differed little from the eighteenth-century 32-pounders now displayed on the main bastions.

Fortress life has always tended to be a mixture of long periods of peacetime inactivity and tedium, enlivened by the excitement of the threat of war and, much more rarely, by actual action. Walmer in the sixteenth century was no exception. The Downs was always a busy anchorage, so there was plenty to see, while foreign vessels that failed to dip their flags in salute might have a shot across their bows from the castle gunners. Faced with a far more serious invasion threat in the Armada year of 1588, all the defences here were readied. No doubt the garrison anxiously followed news of the running skirmishes up the Channel, and they may have heard the gunfire of the final fight off Gravelines, but none of the castles of the Downs saw action, although their garrisons probably remained at full strength throughout the war years at the end of Elizabeth I's reign.

A view of Walmer from the north-east. Beyond the bastion is the accommodation begun by the Duke of Dorset in the early eighteenth century

THE CINQUE PORTS
AND THE OFFICE OF LORD WARDEN

The Cinque Ports seal

The Cinque Ports Confederation originated in the eleventh century when the five original port towns – Hastings, Romney, Hythe, Dover and Sandwich – banded together to provide ships and men for the defence of the coast and protection of cross-channel trade. In return for these services they received substantial local privileges, including immunity from all external courts of justice and from national taxation. These privileges far outweighed the duties, particularly when these services could serve as cover for little more than licensed piracy. The rapid growth of the Confederation and its lack of control became an increasing worry to successive kings.

In the thirteenth century, the office of Warden was instituted by the Crown to oversee the affairs of the Confederation. Later in the thirteenth century, it was amalgamated with that of Constable of Dover Castle. From the fourteenth century, the holder was usually appointed for life, but the monarch never allowed it to become a hereditary title.

By the sixteenth century, the Cinque Ports were in decline as trade patterns changed and harbours began to silt. The establishment of a permanent Royal Navy removed the need for their services as ship-providers to the Crown. However, the Confederation clung to its privileges, until further reforms in the nineteenth century abolished most of these.

In its heyday, the office of Lord Warden carried both power and responsibility, as well as considerable scope for personal enrichment. By the nineteenth century, the Lord Warden's power was analogous to that of a Lord Lieutenant and until 1828 he enjoyed a substantial annual salary of £3,000. Throughout its long history, the office has been held by many distinguished people, perhaps no more so than in the last two centuries, when it has been increasingly seen as a high honour to be conferred on those who have given especially distinguished service to the State.

HM Queen Elizabeth the Queen Mother, pictured on the bastions at Walmer with the ceremonial oar of the Cinque Ports

JULIAN CALDER

Lords Warden since 1708

Duke of Dorset (1708)
Duke of Ormonde (1713)
Duke of Dorset (1714)
Earl of Leicester (1717)
Duke of Dorset (1728)
Earl of Holderness (1765)
Earl of Guilford (1778)
Rt Hon William Pitt (1792)
Earl of Liverpool (1806)
Duke of Wellington (1829)
Marquess of Dalhousie (1853)
Viscount Palmerston (1861)
Earl Granville (1865)
Rt Hon W H Smith (1891)
Marquess of Dufferin and Ava (1891)
Marquess of Salisbury (1895)
Marquess Curzon of Kedleston (1904)
HRH Prince of Wales (1905)
Earl Brassey (1907)
Earl Beauchamp (1913)
Marquess of Reading (1934)
Marquess of Willingdon (1936)
Sir Winston Churchill (1941)
Sir Robert Menzies (1965)
HM Queen Elizabeth the Queen Mother (1978)

The Cinque Ports shield

Inventory from October 1681, giving a stock list of gunpowder and shot used by the garrison

Walmer Castle in the Seventeenth Century

Engraving of Thomas, Lord Fairfax, after Robert Walker

Under the early Stuart kings in the seventeenth century, the castles in the Downs were starved of funds, and garrison morale was low, with many of the men living in Deal and forced to take other jobs to supplement their low pay. The castles themselves were in a poor state of repair. Worse still, the Downs anchorage in the 1620s and 1630s was increasingly the scene of fights and skirmishes between 'Dunkirker' privateers and Dutch, French and Spanish ships. This culminated in a pitched sea-battle in 1639 between a Spanish fleet of 140 ships and a Dutch force under Admiral van Tromp, leading to some 2000 Spanish wounded being put ashore at Deal. The three castles had neither the munitions nor the will to intervene and enforce the English law forbidding acts of war here. All

three castles came under Parliamentary control on the outbreak of the English civil war the following year.

In 1648, the execution of Charles I provoked a serious uprising in Kent and led the fleet then anchored at the Downs to come out in favour of the rebels. Royalists occupied Sandown, Deal and Walmer and laid siege to Dover Castle. Although Fairfax and the New Model Army bloodily suppressed the main uprising at the Battle of Maidstone on 1 June, the coastal fortresses, supplied from the sea, continued to hold out. A Parliamentary force of some 2000 troops under Colonel Rich moved swiftly to raise the siege of Dover Castle, which was accomplished by 5 June, before moving on Walmer. The siege here began around 15 June, but as Rich had no artillery, it was 12 July before the castle surrendered, probably because of a lack of provisions. By then, Rich had acquired a number of heavy guns, but even with these, he was unable to obtain the surrender of

Deal and Sandown Castles until 23 August, when news of the defeat of Scottish forces at the Battle of Preston finally ended Royalist hopes.

Despite the lack of artillery bombardment, Walmer Castle had suffered considerable damage, although less than Deal. Colonel Rich wrote of Walmer to the Speaker of the House of Commons, '...three hundred pounds will complete it. I fear five hundred pounds will scarce render this in so good a condition as it was before it was besieged'. Rich was appointed Captain of Deal Castle and supervised repairs to all three fortresses. These were completed in time for the castles to resume their role of defending the Downs anchorage, notably during the Dutch Wars of the 1650s and 1660s. Although the castles were not attacked, they guaranteed a safe anchorage for English ships, most notably during the First Dutch War (1652–4) when the Dutch fleet under Admiral van Tromp was unable to attack an English convoy and its ten escorting warships commanded by Sir George Ayscue, who had sought shelter under the guns of the three castles.

The Dutch Wars were something of a swansong for the castles of the Downs. Their design was increasingly old-fashioned in an age where the angle bastion reigned supreme for defence works. In 1697, the diarist Celia Fiennes in her journey through Kent, referred to them somewhat disparagingly as 'three little forts or castles...which hold few guns but I should think they would be of little effect and give the enemy no great trouble'. Despite this obsolescence, Deal and Sandown were to continue in active military use for over another century. Walmer, however, was to find a new role as an official residence, although for a time it retained some of its armament.

Walmer Castle in the Eighteenth Century

In 1708, the Duke of Dorset was appointed Lord Warden. Since the thirteenth century, the Warden's official residence had been at Dover Castle, almost invariably over Constable's Gateway. By the beginning of the eighteenth century, Dover Castle was partly ruinous, while

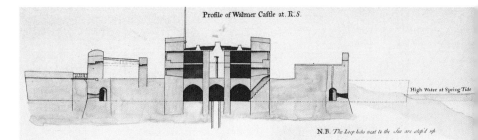

Profile of Walmer Castle at R.S.

High Water at Spring Tide

N.B. *The Loop holes next to the Sea are stop'd up.*

Cross-section of Walmer Castle in 1741

the accommodation in Constable's Gateway was cramped, old-fashioned and probably extremely cold and draughty. Whatever the reasons, the Duke of Dorset chose to move to Walmer Castle which has remained the official residence ever since. This change did not immediately end the military use of Walmer, which seems to have retained a limited number of guns and gunners beyond the end of the Napoleonic Wars in 1815, but it signalled the start of the gradual evolution of the castle into a country residence and the establishment of the surrounding gardens and grounds.

The Duke of Dorset (Lord Warden 1708–13, 1714 and 1728–65) was the first of several Lords Warden to adapt the castle to a more domestic role. He provided extra accommodation by building out over the courtyard between the keep and the north bastion. Perhaps mindful of the castle's need to retain a military function, he was careful to leave the north bastion clear for mounting guns. This extension today contains the main dining and drawing room. In the early 1730s, he had a two-storey, weather-boarded house built into the rear of the south bastion as accommodation for the castle gunners; this survives, partly encased by later alterations.

Although the castle's days as a fortress were nearly over, military use of the area was growing. There had been a small navy yard at

Drawing of Walmer Castle in 1735, by the Buck Brothers, showing the Tudor gatehouse before the additions made 150 years later

THE DUKE OF DORSET
(1688–1756)

NATIONAL PORTRAIT GALLERY, LONDON

Lionel Cranfield, first Duke of Dorset, was a courtier who held a number of high political offices under Queen Anne and the first two Georges. In his later career he served for a number of years as Lord Lieutenant of Ireland. As Lord Warden he probably favoured Walmer for its compact size, compared to the great rambling fortress of Dover. His younger contemporary, Lord Shelburne described him as 'the perfect English courtier and nothing else; he had the good fortune to come into the world with the whigs, and partook of their good fortune to his death. He never had an opinion about public matters, he preserved to the last the good breeding, decency of manners and dignity of exterior deportment of Queen Anne's time.' Horace Walpole, while acknowledging the duke's public dignity, remarked more acidly that in private he was 'the greatest lover of low humour and buffoonery'.

Portrait of the Duke of Dorset, by Sir Godfrey Kneller, 1710. He was the first Lord Warden to live at Walmer

Deal since the seventeenth century. In 1714, the Master General of Ordnance established land and sea ranges here for gunnery practice, expanding a military presence that was to remain unbroken until 1996, evident in the former barracks and naval hospital west of the town of Deal.

The Duke of Dorset's alterations to the castle seemed to have sufficed for his eighteenth-century successors. When George III appointed William Pitt as Lord Warden in 1792, it was with the express purpose of helping the Prime Minister's precarious finances, and Pitt's tenure (1792–1806) is chiefly notable for the improvements that he and his niece, Lady Hester Stanhope, made to the gardens and grounds.

Walmer Castle in the Nineteenth Century

The most famous of the nineteenth-century Lords Warden, the Duke of Wellington, who was appointed in 1829, was delighted with the castle. The hero of Waterloo frequently stayed

here, living simply and sleeping on his campaign bed in his little room looking out over the sea. He loved the company of local friends and their children. He entertained frequently, holding two or three dinner parties each week, often inviting the officers from the Dover garrison as well as those quartered in Deal and naval officers from warships in the Downs. In 1835 he was visited here by the sixteen-year-old Princess Victoria. Seven years later, when she was queen, he lent the castle to her, and she stayed for nearly a month with Prince Albert and their children. In September 1852, the Duke of Wellington died at the castle; his room is shown as it was on the day of his death.

In 1865 Earl Granville was appointed Lord Warden. He and his young second wife, whom he married that year, did much to improve the neglected grounds, reinstating much of Pitt and Lady Hester's work. Most notably, the Granvilles laid out the gravel walk west of the castle, flanked by the herbaceous borders and great yew hedges. In 1874, they commissioned the architect George Devey to build extra rooms over the gatehouse for their family. Devey had an extensive country-house practice and was well known for his sensitive additions to historic buildings. His work at Walmer was to be the last major extension to the castle.

Seal and signature of Viscount Palmerston, Lord Warden in 1861

W H Smith, founder of the well-known bookshops, was appointed Lord Warden in 1891. Although he was a sick man, and lived for only another six months, he did much to ensure the survival of furniture and artefacts that had historical associations with the castle. Until then, it had been the custom for incoming Lords Warden to purchase the castle furniture from the families of their predecessors, and not all wished to do so. To prevent the loss of historically significant items, W H Smith proposed to set up a trust to ensure that such furniture and mementoes remained at the castle in perpetuity. It was left to his son to establish the trust. The 'heirloom' furniture at Walmer can be identified by small, numbered brass plates. Later Lords Warden have added to the collection.

Outside the castle, the communities of Walmer and Deal were growing rapidly in the nineteenth century, largely as a result of the establishment of the barracks. Walmer and its neighbourhood was also a favourite retirement place for senior naval and military officers. Walmer Castle itself was increasingly a magnet for fashionable society, the number of large houses, particularly to the west of the castle, a reflection of this.

Photograph of Earl Granville, Lord Warden in 1865

Photograph of the Marquess of Salisbury, Lord Warden in 1895

Walmer People

MARQUESS CURZON OF KEDLESTON
(1859–1925)

Lord Curzon as Viceroy of India. He was Lord Warden in 1904

Lord Curzon is best known as the youngest Viceroy of India (1898–1905), and as a Foreign Secretary (1919–24), who played a major role in British policy-making during his terms in office. While Viceroy of India, Curzon had ordered the restoration of the Taj Mahal, and he took a personal interest in India's artistic and cultural heritage.

After his return from India, he was offered the post of Lord Warden, and was installed on 2 July 1905. But his stay at the castle was not happy. His wife, Mary, fell dangerously ill, which he attributed to the poor state of the castle, and she was moved to a house nearby in Walmer, where unfortunately she died. Her death affected him deeply, and in the November he resigned the post. After his wife's death, he inherited a substantial fortune, which allowed him to indulge in his passion for the collection of art treasures and old buildings. In 1911 he bought his first castle, Tattershall, in Lincolnshire, which he restored. He subsequently restored Bodiam Castle, Sussex, eventually presenting both castles to the fledgling National Trust.

Curzon continued to be interested in Walmer, and his book on the history of the castle, Walmer Castle and its Lords Warden, *published after his death, still remains the best book on the history of the castle.*

Walmer People

EARL BEAUCHAMP
(1872–1938)

Photograph of Earl Beauchamp on the bastions at Walmer

William Lygon, seventh Earl Beachamp (Lord Warden from 1913 to 1934) was an aristocratic member of the political establishment at the turn of the twentieth century. He was a politically active Liberal peer from the age of thirty, and a member of the cabinet in Asquith's government from 1910 to 1915. He was the leader of the movement to end the First World War by a negotiated peace, and he was leader of the Liberal Party in the House of Lords from 1923 to 1931.

But it is not for his political career that he is now primarily known. His life and that of his family are said to have inspired Evelyn Waugh when writing his novel Brideshead Revisited. *Certain elements of his family life are paralleled in the novel. Like the Flyte family, the Beauchamps were Catholic, and the family chapel at their country seat in Worcestershire, Madresfield, was the model for the Flyte family chapel.*

He and his wife had seven children, and photographs taken from their stays at Walmer Castle show a close family enjoying their surroundings and each other's company. However, a scandal relating to Earl Beauchamp's private life, which his brother-in-law, the second Duke of Westminster, threatened to expose, meant that he had to renounce his public posts, including that of Lord Warden in 1934 and go into exile abroad. Despite this, he remained in close contact with his family, and his children followed him around Europe until his death in New York in 1938.

Above: Cover of the first edition of Brideshead Revisited, *by Evelyn Waugh, said to have been inspired by the Beauchamps*

Some of the Beauchamp children on the Broadwalk at Walmer

Walmer Castle in the Twentieth Century

Throughout the twentieth century Walmer Castle continued its role as the official residence of the Lords Warden. Among the most enthusiastic tenants was Earl Beauchamp. He and his wife, Lady Lettice Grosvenor, sister of the Duke of Westminster, made the castle the hub of social life in the area. Each summer, they hosted house parties, tennis and croquet matches and dances.

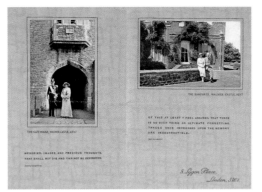

Lord and Lady Willingdon's Christmas card from 1937, showing them outside the gatehouse at Walmer

gatehouse, although they continued to use the rest of the castle and grounds for entertaining. Churchill's successor, Sir Robert Menzies, Prime Minister of Australia, was a regular and keen visitor. So too was Her Majesty Queen Elizabeth the Queen Mother, Lord Warden from 1978 to 2002. She stayed at the castle each year, taking a close interest in the gardens and grounds.

Punch *cartoon commemorating Churchill's first visit to Walmer after his appointment as Lord Warden, 25 September 1941*

In 1915, during the First World War, Earl Beauchamp lent Walmer to Prime Minister Asquith as a weekend retreat. Because of the castle's proximity to London and the Channel ports, it made an ideal location for meetings. Many eminent people were present at Asquith's weekend house parties, including Lord Kitchener, Winston Churchill, the poet Rupert Brooke and the author Henry James.

Sir Winston Churchill was Lord Warden from 1941 to 1965, though he never stayed at the castle. After the Second World War, the Lords Wardens were provided with a private apartment in the Devey extension over the

Portrait of Sir Robert Menzies wearing the robes and Order of the Thistle, by David Poole PRA, 1971, which hangs in the private apartments at Walmer

In more than four and a half centuries, Walmer Castle has seen many changes. Built to resist invasion, but besieged and captured in a later civil war, it retained a military role into the nineteenth century. By then, it had been the residence of the Lords Warden for over a hundred years, a felicitous and highly appropriate use for the castle, given that one of Warden's prime aims had been the defence of these coastal waters.

Walmer People

HM QUEEN ELIZABETH THE QUEEN MOTHER
(1900–2002)

Her Majesty Queen Elizabeth the Queen Mother was installed as Lord Warden of the Cinque Ports in 1978, taking over the post from her friend Sir Robert Menzies, who had been Prime Minster of Australia during the Second World War.

Taking on the post of Lord Warden was a special honour for the Queen Mother, as she was the first female incumbent. She particularly enjoyed the ceremonial aspects of the post, and the close relationship with this part of the Kent coast. She was always determined to visit the castle every year, despite worries about her strength and health in later life. Even when she was 101, she still made her annual trip to Walmer in July for a long weekend, flying in by helicopter.

Preparations for the visit of the Queen Mother and her household included moving some of the more fragile items of furniture from the Drawing Room and Dining Room, and bringing in some of her own furniture from her other residences. Her butlers always took great interest in the arrangement of the furniture, making sure that it was comfortable and to her taste, and very much a home from home. It was in the Drawing Room and Dining Room that she chose to entertain the mayors and officials of the Cinque Ports and a wide range of people from East Kent and Sussex. She also ventured out from the castle and met the local inhabitants, both during official ceremonies and at the Sunday Church service at St Mary's in Walmer, which she invariably attended.

She also enjoyed the castle gardens and took a keen interest in their progress and upkeep. Hence, as a ninety-fifth birthday gift, Penelope Hobhouse was commissioned by English Heritage to design a garden within the castle grounds especially for her.

The gardens were always a prominent feature during her visit, not only providing a graceful backdrop for her parties, but also coming into the castle in the form of beautifully arranged floral displays. In particular, the delicate pink Queen Mother's rose was always prominent in the displays. These arrangements were always left in the rooms after she had gone, so those visitors who were lucky enough to see the castle shortly after she had been in residence could still sense how her visits brought the castle back to life.

HM Queen Elizabeth the Queen Mother in her garden at Walmer Castle, 16 July 2001